The Shout

An Appledore Anthology

Celia Ann Merrill

Published in 2025 by Discover Your Bounce Publishing
www.discoveryourbouncepublishing.com
Copyright © Discover Your Bounce Publishing
All rights reserved.
Printed in the United States of America & the UK. No part of this book may be used, replicated or reproduced, stored in a retrieval system, or transmitted in any form or by any means, electronic, mechanical, photocopying, recording, or otherwise, without the written permission of the author(s). Quotations of no more than 25 words are permitted, but only if used solely for the purposes of critical articles or reviews.

ISBN: 978-1-914428-37-1

Although the author and publisher have made every effort to ensure that the information in this book is correct at the time of going to print, the author and publisher do not assume and therefore disclaim liability to any party. The author and the publisher will not be held responsible for any loss or damage save for that caused by their negligence.

Although the author and the publisher have made every reasonable attempt to achieve accuracy in the content of this book, they assume no responsibility for errors or omissions.

Page design and typesetting by Discover Your Bounce Publishing

The art of linguistic mischief has helped Celia through a wealth of written work. Her inner wordsmith was energised on relocation to Appledore from a landlocked Shire. A former healthcare professional, with detours into Education and Administration, Celia is now writing for fun.

Challenged by an impassioned Yacht Master to write a poem as an objection to an offshore wind farm application, A Wind Up subsequently entertained the councillors at the Bideford Town Planning meeting. With the publication of Potholes, Celia was invited to join the poets in the light verse webzine Lighten Up Online. Charities and other organisations have used her verse; her poems have been published in several anthologies and the press, resulting in a tongue-in-cheek invitation to march on 10 Downing Street in support of the Poets' Defence League. The Shout was long listed for the Plough Prize.

This collection of poems illustrates and celebrates the sights, sounds, emotions and experiences that have been enjoyed in this inspiring and beautiful environment.

Caveat Emptor

Ab fab poem. Who needs Pam Ayres? Sara Spring.

Read Easy

I love your poem - what a brilliant idea!

Ginny Williams-Ellis Founder, Read Easy UK
www.readeasy.org.uk

River Rebels

Celia Ann Merrill's poem made me smile. I am that 'absent 'slipway warden............ I was not reappointed due to the fact that I could not produce my 5 GCE certificates for 1962 despite excellent references and a long career in management …. Yes, Mr Jobsworth is alive….

RM, Fremington, in the North Devon Gazette

Samhain on Dartmoor

Richly evocative of time and place, Samhain on Dartmoor transports the reader straight to an intense autumn day on the moor. This poem makes me fall in love (again) with Dartmoor, and autumn.'

Rebecca Alexander

Try eating a rainbow

I am crying as I read this. It is perfect. Absolutely perfect. I will have some run off and left for the men.

On behalf of all those lovely people out there who need this support, thank you.

Ann Bruce **www.harmony-in-health.com**

Fire & Ice

Poem arrived this morning and very gratefully received. Many thanks for thinking of us and the homeless 'boys' we are very privileged to look after. Much of what you say is indeed true and would ring many very loud bells with the men who are in our care.

Colonel Geoffrey Cardozo MBE VETERANS AID
www.veterans-aid.net

(This poem previously referenced the charity Veterans Aid.)

A Degree of Compassion

I really like this poem, so clever and so true! …Our third book will focus on how to increase positivity and resilience in order to ensure that nurses do 'nourish' themselves and others. If appropriate, could we use it in the third book?

Claire Chambers, Oxford Brookes University. Co-author of 'Compassion and Caring in Nursing' & 'Excellence in compassionate nursing care: leading the change'.

CONTENTS

Prologue

All At Sea

The Shout	2
Appledore Frock	4
A Wind Up	6
A Club Gig	8
Winter Dipping	9
River Rebels	10
Littoral Alliteration	12
Respect	14
Coming in Waves	16
Awash with Words	17

Landlubbers

Pedometer	20
Knickers!	22
A Sticky Business	24
Potholes	26
Caveat Emptor	28
Open Doors	30
However	32
A Pleamail	33
And Lo!	34
P.S.	35
Factory Friday 21.12.2012	36
The Charge of the Trade Brigade	38
My Muse	41
Market Street Kitchen	42
The Coffee Cabin	43
BeauTangles	44
The Seagate	45

Seasonal Reading

Bridesmaids	50
Invitation from a Gardener	51
May Day	52

CONTENTS CONT'D

The Ruby Country Fair	53
Samhain on Dartmoor	54
BREATHE	55
Fire and Ice	58
Frozen Music	60
Festive Glue	62

Flotsam and Jetsam

Dear Publisher	66
Read Easy	68
The Volunteer	70
P.S.	72
Arachnophobia	73
Miss!	76
Public Image	78
The Chairman's seaside menagerie	79
Sunday Papers	80
Try Eating a Rainbow	84
A Degree of Compassion	86
In Need of Nonsense	88
Epilogue	89
Resources	91

Prologue

For those who like words versified

Or prose with short refrain,

Or doggerel in various forms

This work might entertain.

In Devon, here, the atmosphere

Assists expressive arts:

The writers, painters, sculptors

All find outlets for their hearts'

Creations, souls' desires,

Now mine have reached the stage

Of finding form in written word

Before you on the page.

Here's The Thing

Sometimes we think
we don't need a Thing
or want a Thing
but sometimes a Thing
serves to remind us of
places
people
good times
or hard.

So here's a Thing
from Appledore
to remind you of
a happy place
friendly people
and good times
not hard.

The Shout

A frantic alarm, adrenaline flows,
A scrabble for glasses and throw on some clothes.
The keys and the footwear strategically placed
In the hall by the door to save time in the race.

Arrive at the station, quick briefing: 'The Plan'.
They swing into action, each woman, each man.
All suited and booted, correctly attired
In wellies and helmets: protection required
For facing the elements, searching the sea
For sailors and surfers; for you and for me.

Doors flung open wide and the tractor reverses.
The crew say their prayers (but 'neath breath mutter curses).
Then into the boat and away on their search,
Holding on for dear life with each wave, pitch or lurch.
The routine rehearsed again and again,
Our volunteer crewmen will rarely complain.
All weathers, conditions, from mill pond to swell;
Sunshine or rainstorms, like Heaven or Hell.

We landlubbers know not what happens out there,
Holed up in our houses, curled up in our chairs.
Or waiting by water, on shore, watching out
For the bright orange vessel
To return from 'The Shout.'

Did something go wrong? Was a man lost at sea?
Or a boat on the rocks that they couldn't set free?
Will a cry of relief greet the crew on dry land?
With those rescued relaxing, now safe in their hands.
This emergency service, with trained volunteers
Will come to our aid, any day of the year.
Each led by the Coxswain, in charge of his crew
All paid from donations, from me and from you.
A token, he's paid, for saving a life
To rescue a sailor or surfer in strife.
Or a bauble for valour, the effort rewarded
Bestowed by officials, politely applauded.
It's not for the glory, this job that they do.
Compassionate angels, RNLI crew.

www.rnli.org.uk

Appledore Frock

Purl your dreams as you fashion his Gansey, my dear,
Entwining deep love in your craft.
May your warmth in the wool
Serve as foil for his fears
Lest this frock become his soul's raft.

A traditional seafarer's garment with a unique shoulder pattern to identify a sailor lost at sea. It might also have included strands of the loved-one's hair woven within the wool.

A Wind Up

Generators gigantic will blight the Atlantic!
North Devon is now under threat;
Our desire for fuel could result in acts cruel.
We'll be snared in developer's nets.

What price will we pay?
The Atlantic Array could harness the power we need.
But what is the cost of the habitats lost
To fuel our insatiable greed?

Now, what do you see in our wide-open sea?
Only Lundy surrounded by calm.
With space for all creatures
Enjoying the features of landscape that will suffer harm.
If the great London Eye filled your view of the sky
And you doubled its height, you'd be awed.
But two forty of those is what is proposed
An eyesore that can't be ignored.

How can it be green, this construction obscene?
An assault to our seascape and senses.
Our ecology wrecked by the lack of respect
For our Flora and Fauna's defences.

And what of the noise? We won't have any choice
But to suffer the whooshes and booms.
Our peaceful location, the choice for vacations
Will reverberate, echoing doom.

And how will the roads cope with all of the loads
From the lorries transporting the soil
For the building of stations fulfilling the nation's
Desire to consume and despoil?

So the cables they lay to and from the array
Will be hidden and buried from sight?
But the damage that's done will affect everyone
In the process. So put up a fight!

Will our grandchildren tell that our souls we did sell?
And kept quiet when push came to shove?
Sat back and did nought, not gave voice to our thoughts
And our silence condemned us to Hell?

A Club Gig

The Appledore Pilot Gig Club
Assembled on the Anchor slip
To bless and name their vessel
Before her maiden trip.

The winter sun was shining
On the crew, in gold and black.
The Reverend prayed, and blessed her,
That God's speed may bring her back.

After speeches, smiles and thank yous
She was toasted with champagne.
Bright ribbon cut; her name revealed:
This gig is 'Margaret James'.

Winter Dipping

Rolling sea ripples
Underfoot sandy stipples
Blue Tits' cold nipples

River Rebels

Slipway warden absent; needed.
Jet Ski notice goes unheeded.

Jet Ski noisy,
Jet Ski brash,
Jet Ski speeding, swerving; Splash!

Yachtsman gliding,
Yachtsman calm,
Yachtsman sailing; does no harm.

Jet Ski roaring,
Jet Ski rash,
Jet Ski Missile! Reckless! Crash!

Yachtsman flailing
Shore crew hailing.
Sirens wailing.
Mercy Dash!

Slipway cleared; access needed.
'Solutions sought!' Yachtsmen pleaded.

Littoral Alliteration

Skern sunrise

Sunday, sanctuary, sacred space

Solitude, silence, stillness,

Sun, sky, spring

Skylarks, soaring, sweetly sing

Swallows, Swifts, swooping

Seagulls, squawking, screeching

Single Shelduck

Southwest shoreline, surrounding, seaside

Senses stimulated, sandals, signage

Smooth stones, soft squidgy sand

Slimy, salty seaweed strand

Squelchy steps, splash, sprinkle, sparkle, shimmer

Shingle splattered

Scallop shells scattered

Sticks storm-shattered

Shifting, sandy sediment, strata

Shrubs, sparrows, spiders, snails,

Sneeze

Suffolk Sheep, shozen, shit, smell

Sailor, sailing, sloop,

Sea, storm, surge, swell

SOS, signal, siren, slip
Speed, service, searching, ship
Sea-King, seeking, saving, safe

Strolling, sights, sounds, scribbling, sketching
Sitting, slouching, snoozing, snoring, stretching
Sunset, shadows, stars, satisfaction, sleep.

Shozen – Appledore word for sheep poo.

Respect

Without the winter's warning waves
Becalmed, the sea belies
The treachery that lurks therein
And will take sailors' lives.
That flat calm view deceives the eye,
Be warned and heed advice;
Even sea birds rarely stay on water cold as ice.

Deep channels, dark; wide sandbanks, mark!
Strong currents and spring tides.
An unfamiliar course can take the novice by surprise.
If go to sea you must, today,
Despite the bitter chill
To forage and to fish for us,
So we can have our fill,
Then may your charts and ropes, we hope,
Your navigation skills
See you safely home, please God,
If it should be his will.

But should your choice to venture out
Transpire to be unwise,
And found'ring on the sandbanks
Water washes past your eyes,

Then let us pray that rescue comes
With God's speed from the shore,
And each of you survives that day,
To go to sea once more.

Coming in Waves

They roar when they hit, such power, such might.
One after the other, going on, day and night.

They roar when they hit, again and again.
One after the other, relentless refrain.

They roar when they hit. I've done nothing wrong.
One after the other, it goes on and on.

They roar when they hit, where no-one can see.
One after the other, they're getting at me.

They roar when they hit, these bullies, inside.
One after the other, an incoming tide.

They roar when they hit, these words in my head.
One after the other. They've got to be said.
Don't roar and don't hit! We're all just the same.
One after the other, there's no cause for blame.

And now I am rescued, a victim no more.
Just waves hitting pebbles, along the seashore.

Awash with Words

Words swimming, brimming, brimming over,
Cascading down creativity's cataracts,
Descending to the dark swirling waters,
Continuing as sperm-words
Swimming blindly in the pen's inky channel
Towards the light of a receptive page,
Challenging one another for a chance
To create an embryonic script.

Initially there is a place for all, until
Dominated by their evocative, descriptive siblings
The weaker words are weeded out,
Leaving room for the bold to flourish.

Yet the strong need the support
Of some connective cousins for balance.

Pedometer

Most poetic words and the meter I chose
Are affected by walking, and the style of my shoes.

The pace is determined by ground, by terrain;
If it's firm underfoot I might get a refrain
From repetitive stepping, time after time,
With a subject that moves me it's easy to rhyme.

If it's wellies I'm wearing, the pace will be gentle
My movement more fluid, the focus less mental.

With sandals in summer, the pace can be lazy
I dawdle along, and the brain gets quite hazy.

For a while there is time for the words to float round,
Then my thoughts are brought back
To my feet, on firm ground.

My aptitude, therefore, as walker, not flyer:
Less poet, more simple, a mere versifier.
The poet is troubled with these two things:
The presence of feet and the absence of wings.

                        Roberta Shuttleworth.

Knickers!

For a poetry blitz by the writers group
At a village event in May,
The committee requested some ditties
To get the evening underway.

'Salacious, lewd or tawdry,
The rudest poems you've got.
Ballads bold and bawdy
To shock and rouse that lot.'

But a convent I'd attended
For formal education;
Three terms a year for seven years
That's twenty-one, plus vacations!

What did I learn in Grammar School,
Taught by many a nun?
Deportment, prayer and social rules,
Not how to swear for fun.

You balance books upon your head,
And don't wear patent shoes
Reflecting knickers. That's a sin
The nuns would not excuse.

Now if you should be near a boy
At the annual Sixth Form dance,
Make sure you shield your breasts from view
With a hankie held askance.

And should he choose to sit beside,
Ensure there's something thick
Like a phone book, to protect you
From his roving hands, so slick.

Your pleated skirt must skim the ground
When kneeling down to pray.
Wear gym knickers of chestnut brown
Not fifty shades of grey!

***

The words I quote are told in truth.
A *Faithfull tale I tell.
Good Convent girls should heed advice
Not take the road to Hell.

*The late Marianne Faithfull was a pupil at my Convent Grammar school.

A Sticky Business

En route to Bude to visit friends,
Meand'rin round Devonian bends;
Delayed, oh dear, behind a truck,
The trailer loaded up with muck.

So, slowly, through the driving rain
With much exhaust and little gain,
We barely shifted through the gears
As up the hill we tried to steer.
The driver struggled with his mileage;
Incessant rain seeped through the silage.
A line of liquid, green and brown,
Oozing thickly, slickly, down,
Poured on the road and left a mark,
And sprayed my car with something dark.

Now had it been a sunny day,
The farmer moving bales of hay,
Or sheep for market, bleating fear,
Or barley grains for malting beer,
Well, either way, we'd still be stuck,
Though maybe not be sprayed with muck!

Potholes

To drivers on our British roads
(To Cockneys known as frog and toads)
Those readers of the Highway Code
Frustrated would-be Stigs:

They're segregating driving zones
With umpteen miles of traffic cones
Reflective stripey megaphones
We find in student digs.

They're digging up arterial roads
Delaying truckers hauling loads
Their cabs as overnight abodes
All mod-cons in their rigs.

But cyclists in their Lycra shorts
Who've taken up new outdoor sports
Don't bother with the road reports
Then pedal past the queues.

They whizz past all the static cars,
The four by fours and Jaguars,
Ring bells fixed on their handlebars
Ignoring all the clues.

The potholes now are gaping wide,
With little space for bikes to ride.
Unlucky riders fall inside
And make the local news!

Caveat Emptor

We were drawn to this house from the land-locked shire.
It was not what we sought, its condition so dire.
To downsize, a small place, perhaps relocation.
No work to be done on it, no restoration.
A comfortable bedroom and somewhere to eat.
A lounge and a bathroom, a quiet retreat.
A home with one story, no stairs, wooden floors.
Maintenance-free and the minimum chores.

A buyer, no mortgage; we had to move soon.
So looking for guidance, we went down in June.
The Agent, we asked him to help with our choice,
But the house, it kept calling, and said with clear voice:

'Do buy me, oh love me, I need TLC.
You'll be really happy, so close to the sea.

A spick and span bungalow I'm certainly not
I have character, charm – Oh, and damp, and wet rot.
A Victorian cottage is what you desire.
You know that now, don't you? You'll love a quaint fire,
Cob walls that are crooked, old floors that do creak,
Electric that's dodgy, a roof with a leak.

Your Seventies "box" has become such a bore.
This village is calling - You'll love Appledore!'

So what did we buy? A house on a hill,
So old that the deeds had been signed with a quill.
When rendered and painted a bright yellow hue,
The wiring replaced and the door painted blue,
The dormer re-roofed and the fascias cladded,
New drainage installed and some damp-proofing added,
The house will feel loved with so much TLC.
We'll be really happy so close to the sea!
'And now', says the house…
'I've a warm black hat, with a stripe of red.
My jacket is Cornish Cream.
A pocket of blue and buttons of glass,
Sparkly, shiny, clean.
I was feeling so neglected,
Inside I was weeping tears.
But now I'm loved and snug inside.
It's the happiest I've been for years!'

Open Doors

Abertaw, Appledore

Mouth of the Torridge and the Taw.

Her estuary, both sea and river,

She ebbs and flows, innate life-giver.

An open mouth, open wide,

Water flowing with the tide.

From way upstream, through far-off towns

Past farmers' fields debris drifts down.

The logs and branches, litter and silt

Sweep past the boats that sway and tilt.

Swirling ripples that twirl and lilt.

An outlet for the Devon rains

Awash with fare for artists' brains.

This outlet is an inlet too

Spring tides bring up ideas anew.

An open mouth, an open mind

Creative thoughts and actions find

A seedbed here where roots take hold.

Expressive arts can break the mould.

No limits as ideas unfold.

An open mind, an open heart.

There's kindness here: each plays their part

To welcome strangers, neighbours new

Or tourists here who love the view.

Good-natured souls look out for you.

An open heart, an open door;

You'll notice that in Appledore.

However

Just because our door's shut
It doesn't mean we're out.
Especially if a light's on
We're probably about.
We might live near the seaside
But it still gets very cold.
The gas bills keep on rising
And our bank's not full of gold.

So please do try the knocker
Or ring the bell instead.
And if we can we'll let you in
Unless we've gone to bed!

A Pleamail

Oh builder, where art thou?

Today there's no rain.

You said you'd be here, and then went off again.

Combe Martin or Instow? You've got too much on.

I'd hoped you'd be done now; it's taken too long.

Blame the wrong sort of weather- too frosty or wet.

When will you be back next?

I'm starting to fret!

We've visitors coming in less than a week.

Their bedroom's still dripping, you can't stop the leak.

The door still needs painting, the drain to be done;

The gutter and roofing.

Today we have sun!

One day you will finish, and all will be tidy.

Do you think there's a chance you will finish by Friday?

So speak to me, text me, pick up the phone.

Or better still see us, we're here all alone!

(Sent by email on day 41 of the building programme....)

And Lo!

And Lo!

On the 42nd day, they did return from the wilderness,

That obscure place where builders enter a time warp,

A zone of their own,

A worm hole that sucks them in

And where time frames bear

No relation to those of their customers.

Yesterday's poetic offering, transported virtually,

Had been brought to form and taken to that place

Where men gather in the evening after a day's labour.

And those words were well received by others,

Causing the builder to feel guilty for his actions.

And so, on that 42nd day, two of them arrived at the house,

Bearing gifts of goodwill, sheepish apology, and paint.

P.S.

Too soon!

In haste I wrote those lines.

He stayed 'til half past ten.

For back inside his worm hole

He disappeared again!

Factory Friday 21.12.2012

And so, despite the pouring rain
To fix the roof the builders came.
They didn't stay for very long,
And before my lunch, they were gone.

But on the doorstep, Mick said
'Come, we're having a do in the pub,
It's Factory Friday, the drinks are on me,
And I'm laying on some grub.'

By half past three Tone's work was done.
I said, 'Have a drink with the boys.
You'll get to meet some local chaps,
And talk about boats and boys' toys.'

They met in the Coach and Horses,
For beer and food and darts,
And very soon they bonded,
Probably over jokes and farts.

I stayed at home and relished the peace,
With time to myself, all alone.
After thirty years you need some space.
Then Tone called on the 'phone:

'We're moving to The Beaver, love,

I thought I'd give you a call.'
'That's OK, enjoy yourself.'
I didn't mind at all.

By half past nine, there was no sign
(One last drink in The Champ)
Then at 10 o'clock, a key in the lock,
He staggered in like a tramp.

He slumped in the chair,
And blinked in the light,
Quietly mumbled some tales
Of his night in the pubs,
With Mick and his mates,
Quaffing too many ales.

Stay in for the news,
Or a film on the telly,
Or six hours on the booze?
You've now got legs like jelly, old man,
I know which one I'd choose.

But if the world should end tomorrow,
As the Mayans did predict,
Then six hours with new friends, I'm sure
Was the right one to have picked.

The Charge of the Trade Brigade

With acknowledgement to Alfred, Lord Tennyson.

Fifty quid, fifty quid
Fifty quid onward.
Into the Valley of Debt
   At more than six hundred.
'Forward, the Trade Brigade!
Let's do the sums!' he said.
Into the Valley of Debt
   For more than six hundred.

Forward the Trade Brigade!
Only by rain delayed
Only the builder knew
   Someone had blundered.
   Theirs not to make reply
   Theirs not to reason why
   By the seat of their pants they fly
Into the Valley of Debt
   Their bank account plundered.

Roofers to the right of them
Tilers to the left of them
Builders in front of them
   'It's how much?' they thundered.

Dismayed as the balance fell
Obliged to make coffers swell
Into the Jaws of Debt
The balance of funds was well
    Under six hundred.

Flash'd all their cheque books bare
Sighing in deep despair
Tugged at their greying hair
Paying the tradesmen while
    The villagers wondered.
Surrounded by shattered tiles
The rubble in jumbled piles
Gullible and Novice
Reel'd from the knowing smiles
    Now, who had blundered?
Back to the drawing board
    All savings now plundered.
Render to the right of them
Tiling to the left of them
Roofing behind them
    'It's too much!' they thundered.
Too late for a warning bell
Now tradesmen had tales to tell
Of those that had paid so well

And came through the Jaws of Debt
Ignoring the pealing knell.
All that was left of them.
    Overdrawn and bewildered.

Why are they so well paid?
O, the wild charge they made!
    The villager's wonder'd.
Despair at the charge they made!
Remitted, the Trade Brigade
    By more than six hundred.

My Muse

It's the house, the house, a musical house
With rhyme and rhythm and song.
The words in the walls cry out to be heard
They've been locked up here for so long.

The Beares were here for eighty years
Then many more families thereafter,
With chatter and song and stories
Soft whispers and much laughter.

Then along came a couple to love her
With ev'ry intent to stay.
Bit by bit they restored her
And gradually chipped away
At the render that needed replacing
And the wiring old and frayed;
The roof that was letting the rain in
To the room where young children had played.

She returned their love and attention
By releasing her stories and words,
So the tales could be told by the poet
And Old Appledore folk could be heard.

The Market Street Kitchen

The Market Street Kitchen serves food with a smile.
Tasty and tempting; you'll linger a while
To savour the flavours of High Tea or lunch,
Ethical coffee, bright salad or brunch;
Fish chowder, cheese toasties, an Appledore stew.
Lavender scones? Yes! Try something new.

Cheerful, light décor: unique shade of green.
Old exposed stonework, glimpses of beams.
The tables are spotless; glasses that gleam.
Napkins in triangles of russet and cream.
Seek the gem of a garden, a floral retreat,
Delighting your senses as you natter and eat.

Homemade and local; sweet treats you must try.
The Market Street Kitchen sets the bar high!

https://www.facebook.com/marketstkitchen

The Coffee Cabin

Beans! Beans! Coffee beans!

Freshly ground for you.

Home-made cakes and Devon Teas

At Number Twenty Two

A sense of fun you'll find in here,

On cushions, mugs and seating.

Great tasting food, bold art, nice view.

A cheerful place for eating.

www.facebook.com/22TheCoffeeCabin

BeauTangles

BeauTangles for a hair do, BeauTangles for your nails,
Support your local salon, a pamper never fails.
A wet cut and a blow dry, or just a quick dry cut,
Or maybe you'd like highlights to brighten up your nut.
And while you're adding colour
The tin foil on your head;
Why not have your nails done a glossy shade of red?
Perhaps a wax is needed, your brows or just your lip?
Let Polly make you look good before that special trip.

For ladies, gents and children, in a salon close to you.
BeauTangles Hair & Beauty will make you feel like new.

https://www.facebook.com/BeauTangles

The Seagate

The Seagate's on the scene once more
Our smart hotel in Appledore.
The doors were closed, we had to wait
And wonder at the building's fate.
Find other venues for a date.

This ancient inn along The Quay
No longer looks the same to me.
The name's the same, but that is all;
Designer paper on the wall!
New furniture, soft comfy chairs
Bright fabric dyed with coloured squares.
Translucent lamps light up the rooms,
Fine orchids with exotic blooms.

A place to chat and drink and eat
For breakfast, lunch or special treat.
The rest'rant, elevated, bright,
With scenes of old in black and white
Of ships and streets, of people, places,
Local scenes and ancient faces.
A lantern hanging from the ceiling
Creates a warm and welcome feeling.

The fish is fresh, prepared with flair;
The chefs and staff take extra care.
Not just your taste buds tantalised
The presentation feasts your eyes.

A twist on classic fare for you
With European dishes too.
Try puddings with a U.S. theme
Or Irish coffee topped with cream.

On Saturday and Sunday mornings
Hung-over, bleary-eyed and yawning,
A coffee, pancakes, U.S style,
Or Mary's juice will make you smile.

And should the summer sun be shining
Have breakfast while alfresco dining
On forecourt tables, wooden, new,
With seats for taking in the view.

Then when it's time for Nature's call,
Find crayfish swimming on the wall
And recess lit with candles tall.
The mirrors, round, by rope suspended,
Complete a décor truly splendid.

Not just a place to wash your mitts,
You'd think that you were in the Ritz.
Ten en-suite rooms to rest your head
With linen crisp on sumptuous beds.

The Seagate's on the scene once more.
Enjoy your stay in Appledore.

The Seagate was lovingly renovated by Jan & Phil, and continues in the good hands of new management.

www.theseagate.co.uk

Bridesmaids

Green, bright green, spring green.
Spring's heraldic flags.
Nature's bunting, strung across the countryside.

As she orbits her sun, Gaia harnesses its powers
For the alchemical transformation of earth, air and water,
Dressing winter's arboreal skeletons in green tissue:
Spring's bridesmaids.

So what of nature's brides?
Flowers emerge triumphantly, subtly decorated
With golden pollen and glistening globules of nectar.

Wedding beds are consummated:
Myriad insects usher the pollen
From stamen to stigma, style and ovary.
Gaia's offspring swell bountifully with the lengthening of days
Restoring nature's larder.

Gradually, as the globe turns her warmed face
Away from the sun,
Tongues of fire announce a retreat to the winter bedchamber,
And those once-green bridesmaids
Dutifully lock away the sunlight.

Jack Frost may take those who tarry before retiring,
But Gaia will protect her chosen ones from the Ice Queen.

Invitation from a Gardener

You don't need a bird bath in Devon,
For it rains nearly all of the time,
The slugs and the snails in their heaven,
Our flowerpots covered in slime.

The glistening globules of slugs' eggs,
Are deposited onto the soil.
You need to remove them quite quickly,
Or the plants will be eaten and spoiled.

So welcome you starlings and thrushes,
Do visit our gardens, eat slugs.
We don't want to put out blue pellets,
Just plenty of plants for our trugs.

May Day

Should sun be out or shied away,
Man's calendar says first of May.
No matter what the weather says,
Throw curtains wide and seize the day!

Watch children round a Maypole play
Or Morris Men, 'Hey nonny nay!'
Performing rites from olden days.

Bright festival of fire today,
For Beltane, in the Pagan way;
And if we nature's laws obey,
Then new life is conceived today.

When in your lover's arms you lay,
On bed of down or fresh strewn hay,
Look heavenward, give thanks and pray
That should tradition go astray,
Then in our hearts these mem'ries stay.

But nature always has her way:
The hawthorn hedgerows white with May,
The moon will move waves in the bay
And sprinkle bows of ships with spray.

Somewhere sun shines with splendid rays
This burgeoning and bright May Day.

The Ruby Country Fair

At the Ruby Country Fair today

I did not see one bale of hay.

There was a thatcher, weaving sedge;

He gave the sheaves a sloping edge.

But being frugal, I suppose a farmer uses what he grows

To feed his sheep, his cows, his beasts;

Not saving straw for idler's seats.

Samhain on Dartmoor

A soft, mottled, grey blanket enshrouds the landscape
In a cloudy clasp.
A chink in the fabric permits a glimpse
Of Heaven's kaleidoscope.
Below, yellowing foxed patches, beaded with boulders,
Criss-crossed by verdant stripes
Form a terrestrial bedspread.

A gathering of granite maidens
Weathered and waiting
Wear ashen clothes patterned with luminous lichen
Adorned with crimson, roseate brooches.
Within the ring, grizzled Elders send out heart-felt vibrations
Of love and peace,
Their joyous voices magnified by the maidens.

Beyond the circle, dark, hardy cattle calmly graze,
Unfazed by the alien bellowing.
These gentle giants, so in tune with their landscape
That their coats now tone with those ancient stones,
Lick moist rosy noses with wetter, pinker tongues.

Witness the Angel's whispers, manifest in the minutiae of
Ochrous lichen, orange fungi and golden seeds.

A westerly wind whips across the sodden moor,
Around the steadfast tors.
Today the Angel roars.

BREATHE

How do we remember them?

Statistics or brave family men?

Each husband, brother, father, son;

A friend or foe? Yes, everyone

Was someone's kin, not Brit or Hun.

A WORLD War.

Not many, now, one Century on,

Have heard first-hand of battles won.

Survivors, stoic, troubled, shocked,

Clammed-up tight, their memories locked;

The horrors of The Great War blocked.

Called to 'Aid England and Her Empire.'

Journals, film and photographs:

Monochrome, their epitaphs.

The colours of their lives greyed-out,

With only poppies left to shout

In case we are in any doubt.

BREATHE

With the rain in front and the sun behind

A rainbow's colours can play with the mind.

Red blood, Red Cross, Cross of St George.

Paper-thin poppy petals, with powdery anthers as black as burnt metal.

Lovers' hearts, passion, heat, Hell.

BREATHE

Orange Sun, saffron sunrise, golden sunset. Dawn, dusk. Bugle call.

BREATHE

Yellow sunflowers, sun-tinted wheat fields, harvest, canaries, gas.

BREATHE.

The green grass of home, Devon flag.

Green-eyed monster.

BREATHE

Blue skies, blue mood, baby-blue eyes,

Writing paper.

BREATHE

Indigo, deep midnight blue.

Service to humanity, power, dignity.

BREATHE

The violet of sweet-smelling lilacs, described by Soldier Poets in French farmland.

BREATHE

Then, when the spectrum is spent,
The light no longer prism-bent:

White light; feather, flag or fight.
Lamb of God. Lice.
Spittle, froth, bandages boiled and bleached.
Winding sheets. Cold military headstones.
Heaven's Angels. Snowdrops. Ice.

BREATHE and BREATHE again.
So, how should we remember them?
We, the sons and daughters of sons and daughters, whose siblings, parents,
Faced the slaughter;
Of survivors, indignant, wounded by grief
For those whose world turned black.

Celebrate rainbows in the spectrum of light,
Commemorate heroes, who suffered the Fight,
And pray for the peacemakers who seek to Unite.

Dare we BREATHE a sigh of relief?

☦ For Armistice Day, St Mary's Church, Appledore.
Look for the dedicated stained-glass window.

https://www.achurchnearyou.com/church/9034/

Fire and Ice

It really is so very cold. If I could be extremely bold,
The weather is so very dire; may I come and share your fire?

I'm truly not a vagrant, a hobo or a tramp;
I chose to leave my lodgings when I helped out at the camp.
It was a peaceful protest, they organised it well;
But the coppers moved us on when the rubbish made a smell.
I lost all my possessions, what little that I had.
The Council wouldn't help me, and I dare not ask my Dad.
I'm really not a vagabond; I'm just down on my luck.
I fought for 'Queen and Country,' and now I've come unstuck.

I played with fire too often, I gambled and I drank;
My parents cut me off and the army dropped my rank.
Was it really all my doing, or the gods that threw the dice?
I'm surely not a bad man, I just succumbed to vice.

The debts soon escalated; the house was repossessed.
The institutes won't help me 'til my service is assessed.
My partner's got the kids now; I've nowhere else to go.
The autumn was just bearable, but now it's going to snow.
I want to make things better, but I've got nowhere to turn;
It's hard to be resourceful when your bridges are all burned.
My creditors and parents, the Council and the Law

Are cruelly cold hearted and have left me feeling raw.
The bankers are no better; you'd hardly call them nice;
They've frozen all my assets and made me pay the price.

Then the people at the brazier, who'd let me share their space,
Directed me to Harbour, a caring drop-in place.
Those in crisis, often homeless, with their stresses and their pain
Will find food, clean clothes and shelter, and feel nurtured once again.

I'm really not a vagrant, a beggar or a thief;
I only need a hand-up, a dose of self-belief.
I could turn my life around, now, rekindle my desire;
Perhaps I'll break the ice soon and set the world on fire.

https://www.facebook.com/HarbourBideford/

Frozen Music

Frozen music, defrosted by prayer;
Those silent thoughts, offered up in despair.
Received by God, all knowing, all seeing.
Abundant, His love for every being
Upon this Earth, or further, who knows?
Joy manifest, in all that grows.

Temples and churches, stone circles, all built
By hands and minds, creators that felt
Inspired to freeze melodic art.
Crafted with skill, appealing to hearts
And souls that seek sanctuary, where
God's Word, in verse, can reach them: there.

Goethe 'I call architecture frozen music.'

Festive Glue

Do social media have their place?
This fast-evolving human race
Can barely keep up with the task
Of 'friending' those who glibly ask
If they can join your friendship group
And thus another social hoop
Is added to the growing list:
Acquaintances you should not miss
When sending greetings in 'The Season'
For barely any other reason
Than sharing all your daily grind
With the world-wide web of humankind.

So, yes, I'll use the fastest way
Of sending greetings far away,
Saving postage, paper, trees.
And be obliging, aim to please
All those who live this hectic pace
Of life we call the human race.

Yet, gentle souls we are inside.
Our busy lives just serve to hide
The complex thoughts that fill our heads.
We'd rather slow life down instead

And choose to sit down by a fire,
Remembering Jesus in the byre.
A quill in hand, a pot of ink
And take the time to really think
Of what to write, to keep in touch
With those we cherish very much.

Now has the snail mail had its day?
Do Christmas cards get stored away?
Divided into piles to sort,
To write replies? One really ought!
Yet there they are, a season hence,
Those robins sitting on the fence,
Old Masters, Icons, daubed with glitter,
Destined to be nought but litter.

I'm sorry if this does offend
Those organised, traditional friends.
But reader, if this note's for you
I'm dealing with the social glue
As best I can in times gone crazy;
I'm really not so very lazy.
My thoughts and prayers this Christmas time,
Conveyed to you by means of rhyme
Are reaching out to those I love,
Remembering our God 'above'.

Dear Publisher

Thank you kindly for your email
'Bout the printing of my book,
In either paperback or case bound.
Well now I've had the time to look
At the proposal and its costings;
It's beyond my humble means,
Unless I stumble on a beanstalk
Grown by Jack and magic beans.

Having done the calculations,
Just to get things nice and clear,
It's very plain I can't afford it
Even spread throughout the year.

By your very own admission
There's no money to be made
As the author of the poems
Despite the dosh I'd have outlaid.

I'm not so vain, naïve and desperate
To see myself in print
That I can squander any savings
And become completely skint.

Even poets that win prizes
Sell in multiples of ten,
Not the thousands they aspire to
When they use their lucky pen.

I know you offer more than printing:
Some promotion, maybe hype,
Give your professional attention
To the layout and the type,
But I rather think my audience
Of locals and their kin
Is where I'll concentrate my efforts.
So, that said, I shall begin.

I'll try a modest undertaking
Print a pamphlet by myself.
Perhaps one day in local venues
We'll see my musings on the shelf.

Read Easy

You can read, you can write.

Do you have books in sight?

Do you text or email or tweet?

Fill in crosswords, read rhyme,

Make up lists to save time,

Read a map or read signs in the street?

Do you take it as read that the words in your head

Will help you fill forms for a job?

Or a mortgage or loan for improving your home?

Or read manuals for using the hob?

There are adults around,

Who make the right sounds

But can't read a menu or label;

Using pictures as clues

When helping them chose

What to serve up and put on the table.

Read Easy can tackle this problem.

Trained coaches will help with this cause.

It's free and it's local,

They'll teach them a skill

That will help them to open new doors.

www.readeasy.org.uk

The Volunteer

Hello, my name is Sheila and I'd like to Volunteer
As a mentor for Read Easy, you're a local group, I hear.

Where do you live, then Sheila?
Oh, in Appledore, that's good
For we're desperate for a leader
Who can manage Bideford.
A Co-ordinator's needed
To help us launch the scheme
For recruiting, booking, interviewing;
Someone very keen.
It's a volunt'ry position, each week it's just three days.
Expenses will be met, but as a charity there's no pay.

But what about the training, as a mentor, for the readers?
I'd need to cover basics if I'm going to be a leader?

There's a course this month, for mentors,
I'm sure there's still a place,
But do think about the other role
We need someone with haste.
As soon as we can fill the post,
An organiser found,
Then Bideford 'Read Easy'

Will soon get off the ground.
I'm sure it's less than three days,
And we'll gladly help you out…
We'll e-mail you the details,
Just in case you're still in doubt.

Having pondered on the offer, I decided to decline,
And hoped a worthy candidate would come along in time.
I'll be happy as a mentor, let another save the day.
Now a leader's been appointed
And the scheme is under way!

P.S.

But wait! If we're to get this right,
There's something of an oversight.
Committee people, five or six
At minimum, will need to fix
The final push to get things going.
So messages went to-ing, fro-ing.

And then I spied, in details read,
Suggested to Read Easy's Head,
That in the Secretary's role,
If we are going to meet our goal,
I might help out, and take the notes.
Write up minutes, record the votes.
So now I'm well and truly in
Our local scheme can now begin.

Coerced into a new career:
Be mindful when you volunteer!

Arachnophobia

'It's only a spider!' someone said.
Arachnophobia? A state of dread
Induced by creatures that spin a web
To trap and store their prey.

Mere thought of those eight-legged beasts
Devouring flies at aerial feasts
Induce a fright at the very least
And turn me ghostly grey.

It all began at story times,
Tuffets and whey in nursery rhymes;
Taunting brothers with teasing crimes
And their wicked sense of play.

Then Charlotte's Web, the children's book,
So magical, yet I mistook
All spiders as quite creepy crooks
That made me hide away.

Bold tales of Bruce, a Scottish king,
Inspired by spider's travailing.
Victorious!
Now his kith and kin must let these creatures lay.

Then microscopes in science class
Enlarged their eyes and hairy parts
Inducing fear and thumping hearts,
And clammy hands like clay.

While in my teens, hair lank and long
The Who performed a horror song:
'Boris the Spider,' loud and strong
With middle eight refrain.

Young Ariadne, consort, Greek,
Did help her love an exit seek,
Transformed to spider for her cheek.
Are the Classics due the blame?

No rhyme or reason for my fear.
I only have to dream or hear
A tale of spiders lurking near
To cringe and shivver now.
A creature creepy, crawly, hairy,
Tiny really, but so scary,
Of all God's beasties I'm most wary,
Don't ask me why or how.

Yet spiders' webs in nutshells worn
About the neck, her clothes adorned,
Might heal a maiden all forlorn
And cure her fevered brow.

So say the tales of wives of old,
Spinning yarns, not threads of gold.
But sadly I won't feel that bold,
Not ever, anyhow!

Miss!

The words are jumbled up, Miss
They don't make any sense
I don't know what it says, Miss
My mates will think I'm dense.

Let's choose a book with pictures
One with fish or cars
Or dogs or cats or armies
Or spaceships off to Mars.

I haven't got my homework
I thought it wasn't due
I'll bring it in on Wednesday
And leave it here for you.

Let's write it in your planner
Somewhere you won't forget
You don't want a detention
You haven't had one yet.

I haven't got a pen, Miss
I broke it yesterday.
Sir sent me to 'Remove', Miss
And threw the bits away.

I can lend you one for now, Tom
But I'm going to need it back
I'm helping out in Maths next
I might need it for Jack.

Please can I use the loo, Miss?
I really need to go.
I won't be very long, Miss
Sir doesn't need to know.

I haven't got no kit, Sir
No trainers and no shorts
Shall I do it in bare feet, Sir?
It's only indoor sports.

Well today's your luck day, Tom
I've got some that will fit.
You left this here last week, Tom
Your entire PE kit.

Public Image

A blog on the net: your diary yet
It's for anyone to read.
In public domain
Thoughts writ in your name
Via your Twitter feed.

This Facebook lark
No shot in the dark
Who knows who'll look at your page?
So keep it clean, what's on the screen,
Another public stage.

Now if you're a professional
And LinkedIn is for you
Make sure your profile sparkles
When clients click to view.

Clean up your public image
Edit stray thoughts and ideas.
What you thought was a joke
When in jest you spoke
Is there for all eyes and ears!

The Chairman's seaside menagerie

Organising obliging oysters,

Tussling with a musing of mussels

Whilst trying to whip the winkles into shape.

The mullet mulls things over,

The ray gets his skates on,

Putting the plaice in his place.

Nothing surpasses, however,

The pleasure of

Getting all your ducks in a row.

It fits the bill.

Sunday Papers

'I'll go' says Gordon, cheerfully.
'No, stay' says Stella kindly.
She picks up her purse,
Gathers up Gordon's faithful dog Fido,
And strides down to the village shop
With a spring in her step.
Gordon puts out last weeks' papers in the recycling,
Just as Stella had asked him to do.

Ascending the hill, swinging a bag containing the Sunday paper,
Stella meets Roger from the 'Readers' group.
'Same time on Tuesday?' says Stella, hopefully.
'I'll ring you' says Roger.
Later, over coffee, Gordon reads the main section
Stella reads the book reviews in 'Culture'.

The phone rings, 'I'll go' says Gordon, helpfully.
'No, stay' says Stella, nervously.
'Hello?'
'I'll call for you tomorrow at seven.'
Gordon reads the 'News Review'
Stella gets tips from the 'Style' magazine.

The doorbell rings,
'I'll go' says Gordon, monotonously.
'No, stay' says Stella, firmly.
Roger is at the door.
Books in hand, off they go.
Gordon peruses the 'Appointments' section.

Stella is pampering herself in a luxurious bath.
'I'll go' says Gordon, scrabbling for the phone.
'Hello?' The caller hangs up.
Irritated, Gordon takes the 'Business' section back to bed.
He has an early start for an interview in the city tomorrow.
How he wishes he'd taken up Stella's suggestion
That he stay in a hotel the night beforehand.

The discreet diner near the village vets
Takes a lunchtime reservation for two.

The dog is due to be neutered.
Roger is the vet.
'I'll go' says Gordon, nervously.
'No, stay' says Stella, reassuringly.
'Fido Bennett?'
Stella carries in the wriggling pug,
Handing him to Roger, their bodies brushing.

'Quick and painless, I hope?'

'He'll be a little sore, but he'll soon get over it.'

While Stella waits, she reads the 'Travel' section.

Village gossip finally reaches Gordon.

'I'll GO' says Gordon, emphatically,

Unaware that Roger, the rogue,

Has returned to his own wife.

'No, stay' pleads Stella.

Stella reads the 'Home' section,

While Gordon puts the kettle on.

'Appledore News' kindly delivered my papers until closing for new ventures.

Try Eating a Rainbow

I take my tea with sugar, to get me through the day.
I haven't got much else in, until I get some pay.
That's two spoons in my cuppa, with a bit of marge and bread.
There's not much else for supper, I'll go hungry to my bed.
But when I try to go to sleep I'm shivery and cold.
It's the poison in my body, or so I have been told.
So the alcohol is poison, and the sugar's just as bad.
If I could cut them out, then my body would be glad.

I ought to try and change my diet, instead of Custard Creams
A 'rainbow on my plate' would help, especially some greens.
And when I eat spaghetti – it's better brown than white,
Put a tin of toms on top, the colour's nice and bright.

Some hot soup made from onions, a carrot and a swede
With a bit of salt and pepper, is what my palate needs.
It doesn't have to cost much; instead of buying sweets
I need to think of fruit and veg as helpful little treats.

A pound of mince from Londis can be padded out with rice,
Or oats and beans and pulses with green herbs will taste quite nice.
To make it go much further put red lentils in as well.
The food will be quite warming and give off a lovely smell.

Perhaps a bowl of mash with buttered carrots, mushy peas;
And to help me put some weight on I can top it off with cheese.

With less sugar in my cuppa and a lot more veg instead,
I'll feel whole lot better and less cold when I'm in bed.
So I'll think of what I can eat, with very little dosh.
It's not that hard to cook good food, and very tasty nosh.

A Degree of Compassion

To nurse is to nourish, the tutor advised.
Let that phrase be etched on your brain.
To nurse is to nourish, remember those words,
May it be your professional refrain.

To nurse is to nourish, let it be said.
Be aware of that thought as you're making a bed
Or dressing a wound, removing a drain,
Taking a pulse, assessing his pain.
To nurse is to nourish, keep that in mind
As you're filling in forms that have to be signed,
Or dishing out drugs, or changing a drip,
Or bleeping a medic; remember that quip.
To nurse is to nourish, I've said it before,
Be mindful of meals, it's not such a chore.
Don't delegate tasks that you think are so trite,
It's the role of the nurse to get nourishment right.
To nurse is to nourish, I'll tell you again.
His food and his fluids, don't think it's a bane.
The concepts of caring are simple, you see;
Add a smidgeon of sense to your smart BSc.
It's too late when he's dead, what use is regret?
To nurse is to nourish; don't ever forget.

To nurse is to nourish, including yourself.

Your first duty of care, to guard your own health.

But care for your colleagues, they tire, just like you.

Offer mutual support, so they can help you.

When delivering care, make nurture your goal.

To nurse is to nourish, both body and soul.

In Need of Nonsense

I think I need a nonsense poem,
My writing's getting sad.
Some jokes and puns and silly songs
And stuff to make you glad.
Some sparkles and rainbows,
Clowns and jazz
And dancing girls with lots of pizazz.

Then sleep and dream of Edward Lear
And Hillaire Belloc, and all that's queer.
Of Alice in Wonderland,
Harry Potter.
So put down the pen - and the jotter!

Epilogue

Thank you to Dom and Debbie from Libraries Unlimited for inviting me to speak about my writing journey at a session of Appledore Library's Book Talks – it reawakened my passion for poetry.

To my fellow wordsmiths Reb and Mel I thank you, too, for your support, encouragement, friendship & tea.

Many of the poems in this collection were published under the title Open Doors, the Appledore Effect, sold as a fundraiser for RNLI Appledore and Read Easy, Bideford & Great Torrington branch. The 5th and last edition was printed in 2021.

This revised edition is issued to celebrate RNLI Appledore's 200th anniversary. A donation from the sale of each book will go to the local crew fund.

A staggering 2.4 million adults in England alone cannot read at all or struggle to read, but many of them don't tell anyone. Read Easy UK is a registered charity that provides free local support on a one-to-one basis. If you know someone who wants to learn to read, contact **www.readeasy.org.uk**

Resources

If you wish to contact the organisations mentioned in the book:

RNLI

Market Street Kitchen

The Coffee Cabin

BeauTangles

The Seagate

St Mary's. Appledore

Harbour Bideford

Read Easy

I am happy to be contacted via email at
awashwithwords@gmail.com

Printed in Great Britain
by Amazon